Voices

Past and Present

Dedication

I dedicate this book to my parents, Herman and Effie, who gave me wisdom and strength.

To my sons, Antwaine and Adama, who unknowingly inspired me.

To my niece, Andrea "Niecy" who encouraged me to push forward with pride.

Acknowledgements

I thank Bridgette Williams, Publisher, and Owner of Koa Publishing in Manassas, Virginia who accepted and guided me though the process of getting my first book to the public and holding me to a schedule. I appreciate her patience, time, and knowledge for without her guidance I may have waited another year.

I give the utmost honor to my parents for their wisdom and strength. Sometimes it was tough love which molded me, which I value today.

My sons were a big part of me writing this book. They did not realize the inspiration they were giving me as they shared their experiences as young black males in this country. I listened and I responded in conversation and in my writings. They gave me titles without knowing they would become part of or a named poem.

I thank all my siblings who taught me the meaning of diversity. Everyone is different and has their own thoughts and values even when raised in the same home. They taught me to listen to and appreciate the art of listening and not speaking so quickly. My sister, Shirl, I thank you for your knowledge and thrust for truth in Black History. She calls me every day with new findings on facts we were never allowed or taught in schools.

I love all my nieces and nephews; however, it was Andrea (Niecy) who would talk until she or I would drop the phone from exhaustion (because we lived in different time zones) from talking on the phone about each other's writings. She loved screen writing. I was writing poems. I will always cherish Niecy's memory. She battled cancer for over 20 years without telling me how ill she was during all our communications. She always would tell me to keep on pushing my book. Never give up and do it for grandma (my mom) who never had the opportunity to publish any of her writings before her passing.

I thank my life friend Sylvia Ford. We claim each other as sisters. She is my big sister because she was born six months before me. I cannot say enough about this lady who only expects the truth from me no matter how bad. We argue on current affairs and race issues, but we always respect and love one another. She always tells me to be honest and true to my words. She does not like to soften issues even when it hurts her. I call her Ford when we speak because I worked at a prison with her, last names were what everyone were addressed.

Doretha Archies, I can always hear her saying to me, you will get it done. A spiritual encourager whom I met while working at a department store part-time and have become close friends.

This is my first book of poems, but it will not be my last. I often wondered why I write awake late into the night to write but inspired also by my early morning drives. My friend, Blanche Smith, I call her a woman of insight, told me I write in the spirit of last night and the beginning of day, finding and looking for a place to rest. She was right. I write when my mind is at rest and my soul is at peace.

I must say thanks to Brenda Garrette, my "partner in crime". I call her this because we always joined ventures together and it was no different for writing our books. We encouraged and advised each other on our books.

I would like to acknowledge Pam Singletary who inspired me and gave me her deepest suggestions on one of my poems (Bipolar Mind) in which I am truly grateful.

Writing is not my first love. Accounting is my first love. I discovered my love for numbers in the eighth grade from a teacher (Ms. Yane) who displayed her boldness in the way she

taught Math. She used music and movies which to me was fun and different. She was also the first female at my middle school to wear pants. I will always remember her boldness. She always told the class to be bold and be yourself in whatever we loved to do. I write in boldness and truth as I know and have experienced.

Lastly, I acknowledge the world and all its' learning experiences it has taught me.

Introduction

Writing has been my passion since the age of sixteen. It was then that I picked up a pen and began writing about myself and the evolving world around me. Well, at least it seemed to have been evolving. During the ever-changing period of adolescence, my eyes were opening to the real world. I knew love and I knew hate. My conscience was developed, and I was able to clearly distinguish between what was just and what was unjust. My discernment came out in my writing. Others who read it criticized my work, deeming it as too radical, too passionate, or too coarse for the public.

So, my writing of poetry took a hiatus lasting nearly forty years. But, now it's back: more radical, more passionate, and unapologetically honest about my every observation, concern, and conviction about life in America. My hands are unbound, and my soul speaks freely through these poems. Thus, the birth of *Voices: Past and Present*.

Out of every poem in this book, I found a connection to link them together as one. I did not start out to write such a little book, but I wondered if the poems could connect to each. I started out finding one connection, then another until more seemed to join. There is a passion in each poem with a raw truth of its' own. In each poem there are many meanings and interpretations. Find your interpretation. You may take what you want and disregard what you will.

Some poems in this book have an introduction and an afterthought which I felt would convey my thoughts clearer on why I wrote the poem. Some were written because my thoughts were deeper than the poem I could write.

Contents

Effie

Mom, Effie was the glue of our family. Effie's heart was towards loving others as family. Family and friends gathered at our home as a sacred place. The finest of materialistic pleasures were scarce, but comforts of shelter, food and clothing were always provided with love. She often welcomed others to join the family for social and holiday gatherings. Effie was petite and possessed a quiet spirit. Her integrity spilled much love and peace upon others.

Effie, I will always treasure the memories.

Effie, dearly beloved, my mother.

To be in her presence was to know love.

To be in her presence was to feel love.

Tears of joy escape my eyes with every thought of Effie.

Oh, such joy to have known such a wonderful, beautiful person.

Effie's short name did not shrink her enormous character.

Effie held our family together with bonds of loyalty and love.

Effie was a mother of seven, wife and daughter.

Effie was a true friend to anyone friendless.

Effie listened and absorbed others' stories.

When Effie spoke, one could not have received as much from the wisest of scholars.

Effie taught her children to love all people.

All gathered to usher her into her heavenly home.

The crowd filled every seat and lined the church walls.

Serenades of choruses from the choir affirmed a small lady in statue had lived her life large.

We were graced with a God-given mother, wife, and daughter.

Pop

As a child growing up, I did not understand my father most of the time. He was a dedicated and hard- working man when it came to family. He worked four jobs which included an electric company he worked for over 30 years. After working all day, he would come home to farm, cut wood for sale and work at his father's barber shop which he later owned. I understand now how the experiences in his life made him tough. Growing and becoming a black man struggling in a Country of hatred forced him to be strong for his family. I understood earlier in life but now that I am sixty plus, I understand even more, and I give honor to this great man.

At the end of your workday, you always came home tired and worn.

I did not understand you were the strength of us all.

You were the one who carried us all and dared to not let us fall.

As I grew, I understood no one could ever top you Pop.

Because no matter the cause you were always up to the call.

Forgive me for not understanding your flight.

You were a man carrying tremendous weight.

We now know as adults you were a God given gift from above.

And I am sure you are honored from above.

Please know we love you more than you will ever know.

 Unspoken many times, but always in our hearts and minds.

You have showed us more tough love.

Most importantly, you have shown us a Father's Love.

You are loved Pop.

What The Hell, I'm Sixty!

After all my years, I am now given many journals and I decided to write my journey on paper. Though my thoughts may not always be what readers may want to hear, they all come from my heart. I appreciate all my journals. They were some of my inspirations which kept me writing.

What the hell, I'm sixty!

Do I really care about the number?

It never makes me sad or misty.

I am just blessed to be a world member.

What the hell, I'm sixty!

The youth think I am old and stupid.

Stand back I am still quite frisky.

And I can teach you something about Cupid.

What the hell, I'm sixty!

I have served my time for and with others.

And there were many times I needed whisky.

Instead, I relied on my loving sisters and brothers.

What the hell, I'm sixty!

I am here to say my mind is not a crime.

My lessons learned were well worth my climb.

What the hell, I'm sixty!

What the hell, I'm sixty!

Now I have become an expert on people.

A lot better than when I was fifty.

What the hell, I'm sixty!!

You Gave Me a Journal

You gave me a journal and first sight of it inspired.

The touch of fresh lined white paper was waiting for me to write.

Flipping through the pages my mind begun to race with anticipation to write.

I could not wait to get to my writing spot that night.

Oh! The feel of the pad gave me a thrill.

I could barely contain my will.

Just the thought of the unstoppable words.

Words flew around my mind like songbirds.

Thank you for my book of beautiful paper.

My thoughts rush like a fast- flowing river.

The words come so fast like swift vapor.

For my gift of this journal, I thank the generous giver.

Now if you will excuse me for my absence.

I will depart into my world of word essence.

Where I can offer to you my thoughts of love.

Thoughts I only can thank from above.

Where Are The People

Riding home the day I was given one of my journals, I noticed some of the street names. I spotted names of Native Americans, and I wondered about their whereabouts.

Where are the people of this land?

On street signs, I recognize their names.

But no signs of the people remain.

Where are the people of this land?

I need to know what happened to you.

I only see you in old pictures staring at me.

In their eyes are hurt and pain they knew.

I can feel and hear their agony and desperate plea.

They now try again to take your scared land,

Without any regard of your rights or beliefs.

Then they wonder why you take your stand

True to their nature they seek only to defeat.

Where are the people of this land I seek?

They removed you out of man's sight.

I used to see you standing at the mountain peak.

Today, all I see is your never- ending plight.

What happened after you showed your heart-filled hospitality? You were pushed back and further back. Finally, you and your lands were gone. After your disappearance there came an aggressive move to build this country the way they wanted it. They needed help to build so they journeyed to another place and bargained for men, women, and children to leave their homelands without a trace.

Bipolar Mind

You enslaved yours for the mighty dollar.

But they got away without a holler.

So, then you needed another plan-

And the search was on for the darker tan.

From the playgrounds of our motherland, you stole us from our tata and mama.

You never gave thought of our trauma.

You packed us at the bottom of rough ice- cold rough ships in the raw.

Our eyes constantly searched for ways to thaw.

You bought us here to work your fields.

You bought us here to clean you houses.

Free labor you got endlessly from us.

But we were always forbidden to sip of our freshly made iced tea.

Every day you called us nasty labeling us less than an animal.

But regardless of your hate you forced our women to nurse your babies from their chocolate breasts.

Your only mission still was to keep us oppressed.

You only want us to exist in Jim Crow's nest.

Not Happy Being A Slave

The process of stealing men, women and children from Africa went on for many years. The misuse of the Bible was used as their reasons for enslavement. Human-beings were literally kidnapped from their homeland and forced to come to a Country where they were tortured by their now "Christian" owners. Many were told these stolen human beings were happy being slaves.

Not happy being a slave.

Why would you think it was a happy life?

It was a life which took my people to their graves.

It was a life of separating the physical touch of a husband and wife.

Slavery was not a job it was a humiliating life.

In God's name, they terrorized my race.

They used Holy Scriptures to justify their strife.

But still, God showed His love and grace.

We see slaves shown in pictures as happy.

This is your lie to comfort your agonizing soul.

13

Come ask me and I will tell you it is creepy.

Despite your restraints, remember who have full control.

Now, who are frightened of losing their grip?

Now, you struggle to hold the reins.

But you see it is not your grip to grasp.

It is not your mighty reins to hold.

No matter the fight, slaves were tortured without end and sometimes as a side show. Slavery lasted for centuries without end and killed many black human beings who were considered as less than human.

400 Years Is Enough

For over 400 years blacks were enslaved in many ways. I lay awake sometimes and I wonder how they made it through. In my heart I ache for them, even though, I did not know them. I have a deep sorrow in my heart which I do know how to console.

I am sick of you, and this is true.

I do not know why you are not sick of you.

How much longer will you continue the shame?

The shame for which you are truly the blame.

400 years we have struggled without end.

Even though at times we had to bend.

But with every breath we continue to mend.

There is strength in our color called friend.

I constantly think of my unknown family.

I am sure many were sold.

I only know them though stories told.

But I do know they made it through the agony.

400 years is more than enough.

And I am here to say we are not giving up.

Even though the abuse I still do not comprehend.

The more you cut me I become a precious gem.

I Miss You Whom I Never Knew

(The Oak Tree)

I miss you, but I never knew you.

I know you loved me before you knew me.

Your love was shown in the struggles you went through.

Through it all, you stood like the mighty oak tree.

You rendered your torch to me to continue this race.

Unsure if I can honor the fight you have bestowed upon me.

I worry about falling short and causing disgrace.

Am I as strong as my beloved Oak Tree?

When I think about the honor of this torch,

I know I must fight the cause in which I agree.

I cannot just sit around relaxing out on my porch.

I must give the highest respect to the honorable Oak Trees.

I miss you, whom I never knew, Oak Trees.

I know one day; I too must pass this torch as you to me.

And I will pass it to one I find to meet the everlasting plea.

They may never know me, but I too, am a Mighty Oak Tree.

Ancestry Connection

Even though I never knew you I will always feel that ancestry connection and I will always honor you. Even today I feel you.

My thoughts somehow go back to you as I sit and think at night.

I wonder why I cannot rid my thoughts of you.

I toss and I turn trying to understand these thoughts.

Then I realize I have an ancestral connection.

I feel your pain and sorrows of the horrible past.

But not even I can understand how you made it through the torturous treatment you endured.

I try to visualize sometimes but my mind travels to a pointless stop.

I dare to think any further, fearing no human could inflict such torture on another.

Today they say equal and better, behind closed doors, only to strategize more.

Written on paper, equality and the pursuit of happiness is assured all people,

Lies continue to be nurtured behind righteous Christian doors.

It is understood today who is truly equal and who will never be.

My ancestry connection fills my spirit and intellectual insight of my past and future.

Insight enables me to work without fear.

Education enlightens my awareness.

My life, I am assured you will never ever capture.

Jim

With all the struggles and bondage, the enemy always thought of more ways to keep blacks out of society. They said we were equal but used their evil tools to always hold us under. Jim Crow was always at the table making sure we would ever be invited to the table of equality.

Jim, I have known you all my life.

You always were with me on every occasion.

You showed me special attention without end.

I could always depend on you without persuasion.

I grew up unwillingly with you as a child.

And you stayed close to guide me.

You made sure my dreams were in its' rightful place.

You made me this strong oak tree I am today.

Jim, now you tell me you are not pleased with my choices.

Could it be because I now know the true you?

Thanks to you, I encourage others to raise their voices.

I strive now to give them a clue.

You are never out of season, Jim.

You constantly find new ways to approach.

You are seeking new openings like a cockroach.

Like a shining light I seek you out on every whim.

Good-bye Jim.

Jim Crow functioned like a fine-oiled machine. There were and are so many hurdles we must jump through, always seemingly impossible endless mountains up the road.

Moving Parts

It runs like a fine-tuned engine.

Nothing out of place.

It is oiled and shined.

Not a clunk or clink.

This machine will never pull to one side.

If it pulls, an arm straightens it.

Do not start? Jump start it.

Dirty? Well, take it to the washer.

Moving parts keep on moving.

Moving parts keep on pushing.

Moving parts never stopping.

Moving parts never ending.

Uneven parts do not stand a chance.

Moving parts are perfectly fitted.

In place to stop engine corrosion.

Moving parts are always moving.

Souls Cry Out

Over time minds began to change. While you planned for evil, forces were working against even you. Hearts hungered to be changed. Children began to love one another secretly.

As children we were best of friends.

We cherished each other every day without thought.

We played and ran happily about.

Oh, what joy of friendship as a child, before we were taught.

Then the world came roaring in as furious thunder.

My heart nor soul could not yield to the ugly fury.

I wanted to stand and not to buckle under its pressure.

Yet, nasty truth came like a hostile jury.

How would we continue from here?

Why now are we judged only by the pigmentation of our skin?

We used to be closer than twins.

Now, we only look for ways to make amends.

Our souls still cry out for that love once known.

Our souls hunger for that pure trust in one another.

Our souls long for a relationship of love blown.

Our souls will never know the love of a true brother.

Unseen Heart

Lies were revealed and friendships were formed with limitations. Unseen hearts were revealed. Behind closed doors we were friends but in the public eye our love for one another was always hidden.

I give you things I know you only need.

I am willing to help you where and when I can.

Although I am not at liberty to let you lead.

I give you just enough so you can almost stand.

If I give you more, it must not be known,

For the masses will be very much displeased.

It is understood for me to remain unknown.

Because to some, befriending you is more than diseased.

I would like to think I am a good person.

I may not intentionally hurt you.

I may step in sometimes if things only worsen.

But there are things for you I am not granted to do.

Some of my dearest friends look like you.

But I am instructed to stay away.

Even through my unseen heart have another view.

It is difficult for me to change today.

You refuse to help only because of my race but misunderstand

when I refuse to pledge allegiance.

I Pledge Allegiance to the Flag

I pledge alliance to the flag of the "United."

And this is where my understanding stops.

Where one word "united" makes some feel so uninvited.

Where some can shout it from the mountain tops, for others, eyes drop.

"One Nation Under God" surely not the God of love.

Not just one word but four words dishonoring The Above.

For so many it is a place where opportunities are written dared to be dreamed.

Wherein the real issue is greatly shoved.

We are told not to make some feel guilt.

When others are deemed guilty for just being.

How far will the eye of justice be allowed to tilt?

How long will it take before both agree?

I pledge allegiance to the flag but with a different mindset.

My thoughts of allegiance can sometimes upset.

How can one feel alliance when stumped each and every day of one's life?

Why would one pledge alliance to so much unwarranted strife?

My Baby Boy

As a newborn, my black baby boy was considered cute, loveable, precious and all the little baby names people come up with. It seemed in an instant my baby turns of age and receives unwarranted strife just because his skin is black. As a baby he was cute, as a little boy he was tolerable, as a teen he is hated and hunted. As a man they want to kill him just because. He can be killed for just walking down the sidewalk wearing a hoody.

I dreamed of you before you were conceived.

You filled my heart and soul with overwhelming joy.

You gave me feelings I could have never believed.

Loving you before your arrival was not a hard chore.

You arrived all so beautiful.

From heaven, you came so perfect and pure.

Not to love you would have been inconceivable.

My baby I love you just because.

As a youth, you lite my life.

As a young adult, your wisdom overshadowed your age.

Your room easily became a remarkable shrine.

But unbeknownst to us all, your shrine was about to become the all familiar cage.

Your cuteness and achievements are no longer welcome.

You are now targeted and hunted for no reason.

They want to jail you more often than seldom.

For my baby is a black male hunted in and out of season.

Pretty Little Hoodi

Ah! What a nice hoodi it is!

I wear it in the rain.

I wear it on a bad hair day.

I wear it when I am just styling.

I wear it when I am cold.

I even wear it when I sleep.

I wear it playing sports.

I wear my hoodi to work.

It is even nice just to lounge around in.

But a hoodi is never good to wear if you are a young black male.

I Long for A Peaceful Heart

No. You will never understand a black mother's grief and heartache. She is always longing for a peaceful heart. She knows the lies believed about her black son. She realizes the harm he is always encountering. She is always sitting and waiting, wondering if her baby will just make it home alive.

A black mother's heart is like no other.

She constantly needs to make sure she prays for her son.

She prays not because she fears what he will do.

But because of how others will perceive him.

Images of the "bad black" male is put on him for no reason.

No matter his loving and caring character.

He is always perceived as the "criminal element."

Where the white son is always seen as righteous.

My heart is not at peace when he leaves my door.

But do you even give a damn the heartaches of a black mother?

No other mother can relate to such a feeling.

Color of his skin makes him a constant target.

Even though they know their image was created from a lie.

I am so tired of your continuous "Jim Crow."

You spend worthless hours plotting and strategizing to kill our sons.

Yet, you go to your churches claiming all loving praises to God.

In my book, you can only be less than hypocrites.

I long for a peaceful heart when he leaves my home.

I want to lie down and rest like any other mother without constant fear.

But I lie awake with unrest while the hours grow late.

Yet, I still pray for the day you stop.

I Sit and Wait

As I sit and wait, sometimes I think back on my childhood days. It was fun walking to the neighborhood store with my brothers and sisters without harassment from the law. I remember my happy times of early school days. My best years in school were during segregation. Schooling was valued. The teachers cared and loved the art of teaching.

I remember the classes where I was the only black student, and the teachers would point and look my way when slavery was taught. The white students in the class would shun me. The white teachers would agree in silence. I never saw black teachers in those schools. We were children fighting a battle against grown people who were constantly pressing us down and breaking our confidence.

I came to understand why so many blacks gave up their fight for equality, as their struggle became as a river flowing up an old, rugged mountain. Stories were passed down from family to family and generation to generation. Lives were constantly thrown to the wind and their blessings stolen because of the color of their skin.

I should not have to sit and wait.

It is because of your distasteful hate.

I wonder if my black son will make it home.

I sit and wait until he comes.

Yes, I get angry and will not hide it.

I am old enough to call it all bullshit.

My youth is gone, and I am no longer wired.

I have become very tired.

Fright of night, black sickness.

Dumbfounded of the richness of a black man's thickness.

A fake scared smile you give him when he is close.

His presence feels more fatal than a deadly overdose.

I sit and I wait for him to arrive.

My heart flutters to believe he is still alive.

Then, I suddenly hear the key turn the lock.

I experienced pleasure for this night.

For tomorrow I will sit and wait.

First School Days

The smell of crayons come to mind when I think of my first-grade classroom at Aberdeen Elementary School. I see it clear; from the time I stepped down off the bright yellow school bus.

I would rush down the school hallway to my class.

In my classroom students' drawings were positioned around the crayon smelling room, big alphabets and numbers matted across the blackboard but most of all I see my first-grade teacher, Ms. Taylor standing there greeting each and every one of us with a smile and a sparkle of love in her eyes.

I remember the not so far away hallway to the principal's office and our principal Mr. Owens.

He was a stern yet fair man who stood like a giant

His presence was that of an educated black male figure. I remember being sent to the office to receive or take paperwork where the office staff were always respectful yet loving.

It was a belonging I felt as a first grader. I look back now and all I feel is true love.

I Remember

As an adult, I remember my playful carefree days as a child.

Good times of doll play, fake food and playhouse decorating overwhelms my thoughts.

Memories of happiness and sadness often crushed.

But love was always in the mist.

I remember my first years of school.

First, I was frightened then wonderfully overjoyed.

I was welcomed, and most of all I was valued.

There was nothing but great love in the mist.

Out of nowhere came the years of the great divide.

School days became an unpleasant chore.

I was introduced to many closed doors.

I no longer wanted to abide.

My final years of school were filled with more lies as lessons.

I had finally learned my most prize lesson.

In This Country.

I was taught how to hate by the schools.

I learned unwanted hatred.

I remember there was no love in the mist.

Stolen Blessings

In all our stolen blessings you always would tell us we were paranoid whenever we spoke out against you. So many believed you and do so even today. You always wanted us to forget the torture and hate. You always tried to push our treatment under the rug, and you always told us to forget.

Born in a place of freedom and justice for all.

Life for me and those before me were not welcomed.

Now I see and understand the struggle.

Now I understand how our blessings were stolen.

I am yet a senior citizen, and I sit and listen to my father's account of stolen blessings.

I often wondered how he could have been so negative.

Now, I have time to stop and listen to this wise man and I understand.

It hurts to have heard of his altered plans.

I listen to my father as he tells me of how he was called boy and nigger.

Mere children employed as his supervisors ruled over him, demanding for him to do a job they did not know.

43

He worked with benefits, yet strongly encouraged, not to take advantage.

Stolen blessings.

The old man is now totally open as a child.

What comes out of his mouth now will only amaze, sometimes shocking the innocent ear.

I sit and listen to his truth with tears in my eyes.

My heart aches because of his stolen blessings.

But You Want Us to Forget

Even as years past you want us to forget but you always are willing to embrace the corruption which lead to the American Carnage which eventually lead to this nation's insurrection.

You want me to be silent about the terror inflicted by you.

You do not want me to speak of slavery.

You do not want me to speak of my sad emotions.

You tell me I am paranoid, and my story is untrue.

My history is pushed back in the school history book.

None had the chance to look.

You want me to forget my history.

My history is fading quickly.

I hear: "Never forget 911."

I hear: "Never forget April 16, 2002 (Virginia Tech) shootings."

I hear: "Never forget the Boston Bombing."

But still, you tell me to forget.

You say: "Forget Slavery."

You say: "Forget the Holocaust."

You say: "Forget the genocide of Native Americans."

This is what you want us to forget?

Wonder

Woefulness has taken over the land.

I wonder our fate.

Love seems to have lost its way.

Loyalty to hate and corruption reign.

Fake news is a constant claim.

Unknowns and turmoil are visited daily.

Lost hope spills into the streets and hallways.

Intimidation stirs the righteousness.

Grief has overtaken happiness.

Never will all be free of the knee.

Only one will fix it, Who only divides.

Real is fake, and fake is real.

Active military lives bargained for profit.

No one has a voice of braveness.

Children watch and learn hate.

Everyone else sits back and wonder.

American Carnage

We have entered the ass of the party.

More of it reeks of unspeakable smells.

Every bowel movement more severe.

Refreshing never rids the horrible odor.

Indigestion only to good deeds,

Comfort only to more corruption.

Agitation to ignite hate stirs in its bowels.

Needless lives lost to its movement.

Come see the carnage you welcomed.

Only one could create what all write about.

Identified as one of the worst in America.

Negativity and hatred were his only friends.

Anger and destruction were his traveling partners.

Greed remains the only commandment,

His energized hatred is renewed by "Americans".

Insurrection

I heard all the voices say, "I'm so ashamed."

But "why" I asked, you were the blame.

In the mist of Congressional Business on January 6, 2021

You let them storm in with heightened bitterness.

I sat at my desk and could not believe my sight.

You let them destroy without a fight.

You ushered them in with caution.

Others would have known their coffin.

My mind flashed back to 911 in disbelief.

I questioned the thoughts of the insurrectionists.

I once again questioned security.

I questioned the law for some, and the lack thereof.

Voices from around the world expressed their concern.

Many not surprised of the actions of the administration.

Many already knew of the hatred.

This was just a confirmation.

You stormed the Capitol in haste.

Did you ever think of the waste?

Children were watching the useless hatred in question.

Some will research on how this was created.

A sad day for this country many said.

Do you realize you just planted more poisonous seeds?

Another day of infamy we all will have to pay.

Another day of sinister deeds.

You made fun of and labeled some as monkeys.

I saw you climbing the Capitol's steel.

Some single handedly hung on windowsills.

Proof of the obvious ills.

You were warned of the coming insurrection.

You allowed the deadly infection.

You turned the other cheek again from a deadly infection.

While never denouncing your connection.

But even after these ills we will walk. We will fight for our deserved rights.

After We Walk

We must now share our voices and use our voices to bring about a change and not to be deterred by their evil ways. We must not let our voices be silenced at any cost. We have a strong voice, and we must vote no matter the cost.

We have come to a pivotal moment witnessing the death of George Floyd before the world.

Lives have been interrupted yet again.

The world has been shaken to a raw truth or racism yet again in this country.

And we all look at another's worth.

Today, we walk for immediate change.

No more wait and see, which means never.

No more shoving the "change will come" pacifier down our throats.

We will no longer be the scapegoat.

We walk to show unity, to stop the loss of precious black lives.

We walk for our children's future.

Lives must not be deemed worthless.

We walk to stop the bullets and misguided hatred.

After the walk, we must sit down and talk.

Not the "Coming of age black talk."

Not the "We can work together" talk on improving the unknown.

We must have the honest RACE talk.

Your Voice

Never let your voice be silenced.

Silence smothers the beauty of the soul.

Only releasing your beautiful voice makes you whole.

So, release the sound of silence.

Let the babies show you how to be bold.

For it is the babies who speak the truth.

They can make your heart turn to pure gold.

A child makes us long for the innocence and courage of youth.

Never lose your voice if you ever have the choice.

A voice lost will never bring change-

Only the loneliness of no rejoice.

Try the voice and rejoice in the exchange.

The voice is made to make a noise.

So do not try to harness mine.

My opinion you want to harness is truth.

My voice will make you think in time.

Hidden Figures

We have always been the hidden figures. They hide us behind the screens and in closed rooms, but we are the ones who were and are still responsible for the success for whatever the mission. Dedication to hard work comes from the black worker. We build, we invent while unrecognized. Proven to be well-education against others who receive better employment over us because of color.

History dictates our unique talents.

Injustice did its best to crush our spirits.

Dehumanized, but still, we nursed your babies.

Deemed bitches while others are assertive.

Tolerating the voices against us, we pushed forward.

Figures of beauty, we forever stood proud.

Impossible tasks given we accomplished many.

Great names of our struggles we hold dear.

Unusual games planned to divide us couldn't divide us.

Respect is a great demand.

Strength defines us, and love unites us.

I Cannot Write White

While staying with my grandmother, my brothers accidently threw away the first book I had written. Age 16, I began writing. I never picked up writing until later in life at nearly fifty years old. I would always hear "You cannot write. Your ideals will not go over well with others. Your writings may hurt. Your writings may be too harsh." Yet, I hear all they want to do is write about us. So, I will write. I will not write like another, because I can only write like me.

I sit in my writer's corner.

My thoughts race.

I cannot wait to put them on paper.

Suddenly, I hear a resisting voice.

I push my thoughts away one by one.

I am reminded I can't write this or that.

My thoughts are miscolored, I am told.

I must write with more tenderness.

My thoughts roar like a freight train.

Suddenly, I have nothing.

My thoughts are silenced.

My hands are paralyzed.

 I remember my continuous struggle.

I remember the legacy of many pushing forward.

I hear the hard truth of righteousness.

My thoughts rekindle again.

I think: "Why should I hold back to appease?"

I can't write white.

I can only write what I know, live, and see.

Because you are not me you are allowed to write your choice.

Allowed to write anything.

Experience any adventure.

You want me to silence my life and my pen.

"Not now," you tell me.

"Maybe another day, because the world is not ready."

To wait means, get back in line.

I choose to write what is in my heart, as you do.

No!! I can't write white.

I can only write like me.

I can only write me. I wonder at times why there is so much hate towards people who look like me.

I Am Only One

I am only one, but I tried.

I tried to get him out.

Out of the Big House.

The Big House where everyone looks up to.

Looks up to for justice.

Justice for us all.

All to whom this Country belongs.

I am not the only one to have hoped for change.

For change we all need.

Change we all need for a better world.

A better world working together.

Working together in tolerance first.

Tolerance leading to understanding.

Understanding leaning toward love.

Love in knowing we are all human beings.

Our humanness makes us all one.

I am only one who wants the hate to stop.

This sluggish world needs more love.

Our dying world which needs love now.

Unwarranted hatred against our neighbors is the worse.

Different in color, religion, gender but we are all human beings first.

I am only one who do not understand why such hatred.

You confess love for God whom you have never seen.

God could be me.

God could be you.

God could be them.

Who do you love?

No Reason

For the life of me

I cannot go to sleep.

My mind keeps searching for reasons.

I think harder for answers.

From a little girl in an integrated school

To an adult in the integrated workforce

I find no reasons why I am hated.

I saw a man die on the streets.

My heart filled with tears.

I could not hold back.

My tears seemed to never end.

I kept repeating to myself,

This is a man.

This is a person.

This is a black man.

But foremost, this is a human.

The image of his limp body will not disappear from my mind.

He was my son.

He was my brother.

He was my father.

He was my uncle.

He was my nephew.

He was my cousin.

In this Country today,

It could be me,

My mother,

My granddaughter.

My sister.

My aunt.

Even my grandmother or grandfather,

Still, I do not have but one reason.

Our skin is brown.

Stop Stealing Us

I wish you leave us alone and stop stealing us.

You have stolen so much from us in the past.

You hate us but love to steal our best.

Then you sit back and expect us to adjust.

Our music you have stolen and made your fortunes.

Our inventions you have stolen giving us no recognition.

You have taken our fathers to create fatherless homes.

How much more will you continue to steal?

Well, for us, the time for stealing must come to an end for you.

Please do not think for one moment we will let you to continue.

For the fight will not be as it was in the stolen past.

Watch yourself because you will end up in the present last.

You question the strength of our mind and bodies, and you wonder.

A journey so tough, how did we make it thus far?

Look back over the years, and you will find your plunder.

Then you will see the star that you should follow.

Numbers

I was taught my one two threes and ABCs.

I was told to say please and thank you.

But no one educated me on the numbers game.

The game of tough breakthroughs.

A number describes our race.

I have learned the number two well.

Second in line or to the rear I am moved.

Most of the time my presence brings fear.

My opportunities are calculated second to none.

If mandated, at least one is chosen as the token.

Then surely, you say, this is better than none.

At every end, life is a numbers game.

How many will or will not make it today?

How many must make a second choice today?

How many will walk away forever in the game of numbers?

Even in a queen's castle the number is zero.

On the picture show we are number two.

You always tell us tomorrow.

But I will not take my eyes off the sparrow.

The Survey

I had to stop here to write because I had a conversation with someone today and the conversation was you. When we were doing very well in our own city you came and bombed it to the ground and in other cities you destroyed fine businesses because they were black owned. Today you call it rioting and blame it on us yet again. The truth is, you hated to see us doing well and you promised it would never happen again, while you want our greens. You made sure your wish came true by blocking every success we make.

You constantly come up with things to try to find out what we are thinking. The surveys are always on a roll. If you want to know me why not just ask me about me?

How do I feel about this or that?

Suddenly

You want to know where my mind is at.

Suddenly

You want to know what ails me.

Suddenly

You care about me!

You will put the results in my file.

Still, you remain in denial.

You wonder if I am part of the movement.

A survey eases your mind.

Am I one of that kind?

It must be determined for future prevention.

The survey shows up constantly.

"Please complete by the mandatory date," you say.

The survey to you is the only way.

You never want to hear what we have to say.

You failed once again to see this is not the tool.

You prove to be once again the fool.

You refuse to see or digest the truth.

Go ahead.

Turn your denying face for the next thirty.

You hope your survey will show you me.

This will only cause another knee.

The survey again will prove you the fool.

At A Home Near You

While you are trying to find out about me, take a good look into your own home. While you were pushing drugs in our neighborhoods, drugs were entering your homes at an alarming rate by way of your own medicine cabinets. You told our babies to "just say NO" now you equip yours with epi-pens and pass out pamphlets to communities to help yours. Why can't they just say, " NO"!

Take the drugs to their neighborhood, they do not matter.

They are low- life, they do not want anything out of life.

They cannot have feelings that really matter.

You say: "We matter; we are superior and own everything!"

Hear me now when I tell you the true word.

Unlike you who say "In God We Trust"

I say to you every word you say is a lie and absurd.

You are about to see and feel the impact of your disgust.

At a home near you will come the drugs you overwhelmed upon ours.

At a home near you will come joblessness to break your dignity.

At a home near you, you will see what you dished out is not healthy to eat.

At a home near you the world will finally see your ugly bigotry.

Without delay think clear and hard what you do.

For as you treat others it surely comes back to you.

Watch how you continue to make others grieve.

For what you do to others will stop at a home near you.

While you still push us down there is a movement not controlled by you or me. A movement which will bring about the unthinkable. This movement will be energized and greater than you or us. There will come a time when the choice can only be that of one.

What Side

I see you today with a different side.

I wonder if you know who you are today.

You question your very being trying to figure out your way.

You try desperately to take it all in stride.

Where do you really belong in a racist world?

Your heart is true, your soul is pure, but your mind is unsure.

You can only hope we see you as a transforming precious pearl,

Rather than disgraceful, unacceptable, or obscure.

Sure, I am both, and maybe more of you.

I was created out of love just like you.

My skin is black, brown, red, yellow, and white-

All colors of love in God's holy sight.

What side do I choose to be this day?

I prefer to be me, just do not push me away.

I am many parts of your one, so let me stay.

Can we please just be one today?

Caramel Baby

Giggle, giggle, giggle-I caught your faint voices.

Oh, that is your brown baby. Again, you both giggle.

From a distance, my mind began to sizzle.

I realized from the tone one's dismay over their child's choices.

My mind wandered as my daily duties became a diminishing concern.

First, the question of ear color. Now the giggle, giggle.

Frightening thoughts of isolation for this child rushed through my mind.

Another caramel baby's life will be cold, brittle, and confused.

With a mother of color and a father the lack there- of,

Parents now struggle between choices of black or white and love or hate.

Grands of both wishing for an opposite mate.

No matter the cost, no one can dispute this glorious Caramel Baby of love.

Grands have been thrown into another class.

Love has joined two people to make one Caramel Baby.

Grands wonder now if they are up to the task.

They think deep but must remain loyal to the class of ass.

Make Our Yesterday Better Today

We can be better than yesterday.

Let us make our yesterday better today.

Let us prove our love for one another not stronger but great.

Prove our hate from yesterday will turn to love today.

Remember the hard times when we were terrorized.

I thank God for in those times you survived.

Today my yesterday was in disarray.

But today my yesterday is better today.

Let us go back in time and pull up our best.

Let us go back in time and pull up our worst.

Our best moments bring about the greatest joy expressed.

Our worst moments show us how we were cursed.

In our yesterday we dreamed of our tomorrow.

Though our sight for tomorrow we can plan a brighter today.

And from the dreams of yesterday we borrow love and sorrow.

But today we can make our yesterday better today.

Living Off the Grass Seeds
(Seeds Planted)

Babies know from where you came.

The freedoms you enjoy today,

Comes from the sweat and tears of a heavy hand.

But your loving fathers and mothers did not stray.

Never disrespect your fore-fighters for it is they who died for you.

Your freedoms did not just come out of the blue.

The blood of true love was shed for you.

So instead of disrespect, how about a hearty thank-you!

You are living off the grass seeds of your elders.

Show your love by striving to be and to do your best.
 Know they fought and died for you, and it is essential to pass this test.

For we can do no less than our diligent ancestors.

Always remember if it were not for strong seeds planted,

Today, we would not have the rights and freedoms granted.

Forever remember we are the vibrant green healthy strong grass.

As a result of the seeds planted, torrid and grown; let us forever last.

The Biographical Poem of E.B. Love

Is organized thoughtful creative and smart

Determined, strong, and caring

Who is proud of her family, heritage, and her accomplishments

Daughter of Herman and Effie

Sister of Herman Jr., Shirl, Dirik, Perry, Stevie, and Bernita

Mother of two sons Antwaine (wife-Summer) and Adama

Grandmother of four granddaughters Autumn, Amaya, Aaryn, and Alana

Who values good education and equality

Who graduated with two master's degrees

Who hates the hand of discrimination

Loves to listen, read, and write poetry

Loves daily inspirational drives

Loves to stand for her beliefs and voice her opinions on current events

Who fears the world of racism will never end and some will never reach their full potential, our children will not escape the dreaded "stolen blessings."

www.ingramcontent.com/pod-product-compliance
Lightning Source LLC
Chambersburg PA
CBHW060338130626
46553CB00003B/1049